D1522955

Cinco de Mayo

by L. L. Owens
illustrated by Holli Conger

Content Consultant: Dr. Pamela R. Frese
Professor of Anthropology, College of Wooster

magic
wagon

visit us at www.abdopublishing.com

Text by L. L. Owens
Illustrations by Holli Conger
Edited by Jill Sherman and Mari Kesselring
Interior layout and design by Becky Daum
Cover design by Becky Daum
Special thanks to cultural consultant Daniel Chávez, University of Virginia

Library of Congress Cataloging-in-Publication Data
Owens, L. L.
  Cinco de Mayo / by L.L. Owens ; illustrated by Holli Conger ; content consultant, Pamela R. Frese.
      p. cm. — (Cultural holidays)
   Includes index.
   ISBN 978-1-60270-602-6
   1. Cinco de Mayo (Mexican holiday)—Juvenile literature. 2. Mexico—Social life and customs—Juvenile literature. I. Frese, Pamela R. II. Conger, Holli. III. Title.
   F1233.O94 2010
   394.262—dc22
                          2008050555

Table of Contents

What Is Cinco de Mayo?

Cinco de Mayo is a Mexican holiday. It honors a military success from Mexico's past. Every year on May 5, people celebrate Cinco de Mayo. The name means "fifth of May."

Cinco de Mayo's Story

The Cinco de Mayo holiday began in Mexico. It started in 1862 after the Battle of Puebla. The day honors the Mexican army's victory over the French.

Before this battle, France, England, and Spain had loaned money to Mexico. But Mexico was bankrupt. It had been hard hit by war. So, the countries planned to attack Mexico as a group. They sent their armies by ship to the eastern coast of Mexico.

Benito Juárez was Mexico's president. He knew his army was too small. He tried to make a deal with the enemy leaders. England and Spain agreed not to fight. But the French wanted their money. If they couldn't have it, they would try to take over Mexico.

Benito Juárez was Mexico's president from 1858 to 1863. He became president again in 1867. Juárez was president until he died in 1872.

The French started marching from Veracruz to Mexico City. They had more than 6,000 men. Soon, they reached Puebla. This town was only 100 miles (160 km) from Mexico City.

President Juárez decided that Mexico would fight back. He had the Mexican army waiting in Puebla to fight. The Mexican army had just 5,000 men.

On May 5, General Ignacio Zaragoza led the Mexican army against the French. The Mexicans knew their land. They knew how to fight on it. The story goes that during the battle, Zaragoza let loose a stampede of cattle. France suffered nearly five times more injuries and deaths than Mexico that day. This battle became known as the Battle of Puebla.

Mexican Pride

Mexico's victory in the Battle of Puebla gave its army pride. But the war was not over. The French named Emperor Maximilian of Austria to be Mexico's new ruler. Mexico continued to fight France. After five long years, Mexico won the war.

During the French rule of Mexico, the United States was fighting its Civil War. President Abraham Lincoln sided with Mexico. However, there were no U.S. troops that could be sent to help Mexico.

The Battle of Puebla showed the strength of Mexico. The Mexican people would not give up. That spirit is at the heart of Cinco de Mayo. Today, the holiday is honored throughout Mexico.

The Mexican flag is an important part of Cinco de Mayo. It contains three stripes. The stripes are colored green, white, and red. In the center is an eagle. The eagle is standing on a cactus. This is the national coat of arms.

The City of Puebla

The city of Puebla is a great place to be for Cinco de Mayo. Puebla's nickname is Angelópolis. It means "city of the angels." It's the capital city of the Mexican state called Puebla. And it's one of North America's oldest cities.

Los Angeles, California, is known as the "city of angels." In 1531, Puebla's original name was La Puebla de los Ángeles.

Puebla is surrounded by mountains. In the late nineteenth century, many people from other countries moved to Puebla. They came from Germany, Spain, and Italy. It's an exciting place to live. It is fun to visit, too!

In Puebla, you can visit the famous battle site. On Cinco de Mayo the city has a military parade. Lots of traditional foods are sold in street stands.

Celebrations Today

There are many ways to enjoy Cinco de Mayo. Several parties are held in the United States. There is a Cinco de Mayo festival in Los Angeles. Up to 500,000 people go to this event each year. Other big events happen across the country.

Mariachi music is part of the festival. A mariachi band has eight members. Three people play violins. Two people play different types of guitars. Two people play trumpets. One person plays a small bass. Mariachi musicians dress in colorful Mexican *charro*, or cowboy, outfits. They also wear *sombreros,* or Mexican cowboy hats.

Along with music, Mexican food can be found at Cinco de Mayo. Some foods to enjoy are tacos, corn, and tostadas. Common drinks are limeade and *horchata* water.

You might also see Mexican folk dancing and parades. At some events people act out the Battle of Puebla. Everyone is honoring the Mexican heritage.

Recipes and Songs

Enjoy these tasty treats for Cinco de Mayo!
Be sure to make these with an adult.

Mexican Limeade

Ingredients:
3 quarts water
6 limes, washed
1 cup sugar
ice

Directions:
1. Pour water into a pitcher.
2. Slice five of the limes in half and squeeze the juice into the water.
3. Add the sugar and stir to mix.
4. Slice the remaining lime into thin circles. Float the slices in the limeade.
5. Cover the pitcher. Refrigerate it for several hours, until cold.
6. Serve the limeade over ice.

Horchata Water

Ingredients:
6 tablespoons uncooked rice
1 1/4 cups blanched almonds
1 one-inch cinnamon stick
3 two-inch strips of lime zest
4 cups water, divided
1 cup sugar

Directions:
1. Use a blender to grind rice until smooth. Combine the rice with the almonds, cinnamon stick, and lime zest. Let this mixture stand overnight.
2. Blend the mixture again until it is smooth. Add two cups of water. Blend for a few seconds.
3. Line a large sieve with cheesecloth. Place the sieve over a mixing bowl. While stirring the rice mixture, pour it into the sieve. Liquid will run through the sieve and into the mixing bowl.
4. Remove the sieve. Add two cups of water to the liquid in the mixing bowl. Stir in sugar. Add some water if the mixture is thick. Cover and refrigerate.
5. Serve with ice.

Teach your friends about Cinco de Mayo by singing "Cinco de Mayo Song." The words are sung to the tune of "Pop Goes the Weasel."

Cinco de Mayo Song

France invaded Mexico
In 1862.
The French were brave and powerful.
Cinco de Mayo!

The leader of the Mexicans
Was General Zaragoza.
He was smarter than the French.
Cinco de Mayo!

It was the fifth of May
In 1862.
The French lost. The Mexicans won.
Cinco de Mayo!

Glossary

bankrupt—legally lacking funds needed to pay off money owed.

cactus—a leafless plant with prickly spines.

coat of arms—a design on a shield that represents a family, a university, a city, or a country.

injury—a wound.

stampede—a rush of frightened animals.

tradition—customs, ideas, and beliefs handed down from one generation to the next.

On the Web

To learn more about Cinco de Mayo, visit ABDO Group online at **www.abdopublishing.com**. Web sites about Cinco de Mayo are featured on our Book Links page. These links are routinely monitored and updated to provide the most current information available.

Index